HI GOD
(IT'S ME AGAIN)

THOUGHTS THAT HELP ME TALK TO
THE GOD WHO CREATED ME

JOURNAL & STUDY GUIDE

TABLE OF CONTENTS

I MISS YOU, GOD

(DEVOTIONAL PAGE 5)

DATE:_____

Hi God —

Sometimes, I run around so frantically trying to get things done that I don't actually stop and DO anything spiritual. I AM "spiritual" but not spending much time with the Spirit.

HERE ARE SOME THINGS THAT I'VE ALLOWED TO DISTRACT ME FROM SPENDING QUALITY TIME WITH YOU:

1. _____

2. _____

3. _____

4. _____

5. _____

That's not how I want to live my life. I'm not going to settle for how things are. When I take ONE step toward You…You take TEN steps toward me!

SO, HERE ARE SOME IDEAS ON HOW I CAN GET CLOSER TO YOU AND NOT LET THINGS DISTRACT ME:

1. _____

2. _____

3. _____

4. _____

5. _____

AND WHILE I'M HERE, GOD, I'D JUST LIKE TO TELL YOU...

_____

_____

_____

_____

_____

God, I want You in my life SO badly, but I have to make the FIRST move. I want to spend more time, each day, talking with You, reading my Bible, writing in my journal and just getting to know You better.

My Prayer Thoughts

_____

_____

_____

_____

_____

_____

_____

_____

_____

_____

_____

_____

_____

_____

_____

_____

_____

_____

_____

_____

_____

_____

_____

_____

_____

_____

_____

FOR ADDITIONAL STUDY, SEE JAMES 4:8, PSALM 62:1

HOW DO I FIND PEACE?

(DEVOTIONAL PAGE 9)

DATE:_____

Hi God –

God, I call on You. I lean into You. I have all this…STUFF…that's bothering me and keeping me up at night. Instead of thinking about all this junk, I commit to thinking about You.

Your promise says that You will keep me in PERFECT PEACE when my mind stays on You. Not just peace, PERFECT peace and inner calm. Just the sound of those words soothes my soul!

HERE ARE SOME THINGS THAT I'M GOING TO TURN OVER TO YOU:

1. _____

2. _____

3. _____

4. _____

5. _____

I should know by now that when I don't have peace, I need to just HOLD ON a second. I need to get You involved. Instead, I try to steamroll through it...then wonder why everything is going haywire!

NO PEACE...NO GO! HERE ARE SOME THINGS THAT I DON'T HAVE PEACE ABOUT, YET:

1. _____

2. _____

3. _____

4. _____

5. _____

God, let Your perfect peace rest in me.

AND WHILE I'M HERE, GOD, I'D JUST LIKE TO TELL YOU...

_____

_____

_____

_____

_____

My Prayer Thoughts

_____

_____

_____

_____

_____

_____

_____

_____

_____

_____

_____

_____

_____

_____

_____

_____

_____

_____

_____

_____

_____

_____

_____

_____

_____

_____

FOR ADDITIONAL STUDY, SEE ISAIAH 26:3, ISAIAH 55:12, 1 PETER 5:7

I WILL ASK

(DEVOTIONAL PAGE 13)

DATE:_____

Hi God –

I can't imagine how these things will happen. They seem IMPOSSIBLE from what I can see. But it's not my job to make it happen. It's just my job to BELIEVE IT! I'm the believer and You're the performer. Miracles are Your expertise. You're just waiting for ME to ask so that You can move!

Father, according to your commands and according to your decrees, I ASK! Not shy and timid, but bold and confident that I am pleasing You by bringing You my request in FAITH!

RIGHT NOW, I ASK YOU FOR:

1. _____

2. _____

3. _____

4. _____

5. _____

Usually, even on a day when I'm feeling pretty good, I would stop there. But, holding back—limits You. I don't want to be the one who puts the brakes on Your power, God!

**I WON'T BE SHY. I WON'T LIMIT YOU. I'M ALSO
ASKING YOU FOR:**

1. _____

2. _____

3. _____

4. _____

5. _____

AND WHILE I'M HERE, GOD, I'D JUST LIKE TO TELL YOU...

_____

_____

_____

_____

_____

My Prayer Thoughts

_____

_____

_____

_____

_____

_____

_____

_____

_____

_____

_____

_____

_____

_____

_____

_____

_____

_____

_____

_____

_____

_____

_____

_____

_____

_____

For additional study, see Hebrews 11:6, Mark 11:23-24

MY GREATEST ASSET

(DEVOTIONAL PAGE 17)

DATE:_____

Hi God –

My ATTITUDE is one of my greatest assets! When people get around me, they suddenly start to feel better. I'm believing and acting the way You want me to believe and act.

HERE'S HOW TO LET MY POSITIVE ATTITUDE SHOW:

1. _____

2. _____

3. _____

4. _____

5. _____

And that goes for me, too. I encourage MYSELF in the Lord. When I remember what You think of me, it's easy to have a good outlook because I reflect You!

HERE ARE THINGS YOU SAY ABOUT ME:

1. _____

2. _____

3. _____

4. _____

5. _____

AND WHILE I'M HERE, GOD, I'D JUST LIKE TO TELL YOU...

_____

_____

_____

_____

My attitude is contagious! I can be a thermostat in the room and set the climate, instead of a thermometer that says what's already in the room.

My Prayer Thoughts

_____

_____

_____

_____

_____

_____

_____

_____

_____

_____

_____

_____

_____

For additional study, see Proverbs 3:13, 17:22, 1 Samuel 30:6

· · ● · ·

THE BEST VERSION OF ME

(DEVOTIONAL PAGE 21)

DATE:_____

Hi God –

I've tried reading self-help books, listening to podcasts and controlling my attitude. I tried to be a better person, but I still have so far to go. I can only do so much by myself. I NEED YOU! But I haven't necessarily "looped you in" too much.

HERE ARE SOME THINGS I'VE TRIED TO IMPROVE ON BY MYSELF:

1. _____

2. _____

3. _____

4. _____

5. _____

I've been asking "what" and "how." But the best version of me comes out *when*. When I put You in control of my life! When my heart is seeking You or my mind is thinking about You. When I'm doing my best to recall what You say, instead of what my critics or my own doubting head says. When I'm trusting Your Word and having faith. When I follow You instead of trying to do it my way. Then You give me the ear of the people who shouldn't listen to me and opportunities I know I don't deserve!

I ASK FOR YOUR HELP, IN THESE AREAS, TO MAKE ME BETTER:

1. _____

2. _____

3. _____

4. _____

5. _____

My Prayer Thoughts

_____

_____

_____

_____

_____

_____

_____

_____

_____

_____

_____

_____

_____

_____

_____

_____

_____

_____

_____

_____

_____

_____

_____

_____

_____

_____

FOR ADDITIONAL STUDY, SEE DEUTERONOMY 4:29, PSALM 143:10

THIS IS BIG

(DEVOTIONAL PAGE 25)

DATE:_____

Hi God –

If I want victory, I have to stop staring at my Goliath and start trusting You for the answer. I have to let go and let God be God in my life. The only way to defeat this monster is to turn my secret weapon loose, and that's You.

HERE ARE THE GIANTS IN MY LIFE THAT I RELEASE AND GIVE TO YOU TODAY:

1. _____

2. _____

3. _____

4. _____

5. _____

What I see as a mountain, You see as an OPPORTUNITY to prove Your power. You not only move the mountain, You pulverize the mountain into particles so small…they just blow away. You give me the VERY mountain that tried to stop me, as my own. I occupy it as a victor!

PRAISE IS FAITH IN ACTION. HERE ARE THINGS I WILL SAY TO YOU IN PRAISE, BELIEVING THAT THE VICTORY IS ON THE WAY!

1. _____

2. _____

3. _____

4. _____

5. _____

AND WHILE I'M HERE, GOD, I'D JUST LIKE TO TELL YOU…

_____

_____

_____

_____

_____

My Prayer Thoughts

_____

_____

_____

_____

_____

_____

_____

_____

_____

_____

_____

_____

_____

_____

_____

_____

_____

_____

_____

_____

_____

_____

_____

_____

_____

_____

For additional study, see Psalms 77:14, 89:8, 145:3

LIVING STRONG

(DEVOTIONAL PAGE 29)

DATE:_____

Hi God –

I know that I could be a lot healthier if I made a few changes to my habits. But I'm kind of weak when it comes to having any willpower. I need You, God, to give me the strength to resist the temptations that I face every day. You said You would satisfy my mouth with good things. I am breaking my junk food addiction right now, in Jesus' name.

HERE ARE SOME THINGS THAT I SHOULD EAT AND DRINK TO BE HEALTHIER:

1. _____

2. _____

3. _____

4. _____

5. _____

God, I want to seek you early in the day. I want to walk around the block with You. I want to talk with You on the treadmill. I want You to go with me when I do the laundry, walk the dog or mow the yard. I will enjoy doing extra physical activities if I know I have You right there with me!

THESE ARE SOME ACTIVITIES THAT I CAN ADD TO MY ROUTINE TO LIVE LONGER AND STRONGER:

1. _____

2. _____

3. _____

4. _____

5. _____

"With long life will I satisfy him, and shew him my salvation."
— Psalm 91:16 (NKJV)

I WILL MAKE DAILY CONFESSIONS LIKE THESE OVER MY BODY:

- I will be satisfied walking on two strong legs, all the days of my life.
- I am satisfied when I eat healthy foods.
- I will be satisfied sleeping soundly and waking up renewed.
- I will be satisfied with a strong heart and lungs that beat well and breathe easily all of my days.
- I will be satisfied with joints that bend and move free of pain.

My Prayer Thoughts

_____

_____

_____

_____

_____

_____

_____

_____

_____

_____

_____

_____

_____

_____

_____

_____

_____

_____

_____

_____

_____

_____

_____

_____

_____

_____

_____

_____

_____

FOR ADDITIONAL STUDY, SEE PSALM 91:16, PROVERBS 4:21-22, MATTHEW 8:17

• • • ● ● • •

LITTLE FOXES

(DEVOTIONAL PAGE 33)

DATE:_____

Hi God –

THESE ARE THINGS THAT I USED TO DO WHEN CONFRONTED WITH A PROBLEM:

1. _____

2. _____

3. _____

4. _____

5. _____

Instead of doing all that, I should really be going straight to YOU: my Father, the One with the answers, the Creator of my soul, my rock, my fortress, my hiding place, and the One who makes me look good. I need a whole lot less of ME, and a whole lot more of YOU!

THESE ARE NEW, GOD-INSPIRED, HEALTHIER THINGS I CAN DO WHEN A PROBLEM COMES:

1. _____

2. _____

3. _____

4. _____

5. _____

It should be the obvious answer for me! Ask You for what You AL-READY know, and You'll never leave me in the dark. Why haven't I been asking You for Your wisdom?

RIGHT NOW, I ASK FOR YOUR WISDOM ABOUT...

_____

_____

_____

_____

_____

My Prayer Thoughts

FOR ADDITIONAL STUDY, SEE 1 CORINTHIANS 3:16, ISAIAH 1:19

● ● ● ● ● ● ●

I AM BLESSED

(DEVOTIONAL PAGE 37)

DATE:_____

Hi God –

Nobody likes to be taken for granted...and that includes You. You have blessed me with so many things that I just take in stride. Not today, God!

THESE ARE BLESSINGS YOU'VE GIVEN ME THAT I'VE BEEN OVERLOOKING:

1. _____

2. _____

3. _____

4. _____

5. _____

God, You've blessed me so that I can be a blessing to others. I've given to Your work. I'm thankful that Your Word says that the "windows of heaven" are open and You're pouring out a BLESSING for me that I can't contain. Let it RAIN! You bless me so that I can continue to bless You and others.

THESE ARE NEW WAYS THAT I CAN BE A BLESSING TO OTHERS:

1. _____

2. _____

3. _____

4. _____

5. _____

LORD, THESE ARE THINGS THAT I'M ASKING YOU TO BLESS IN MY LIFE...

_____

_____

_____

"If you fully obey the Lord your God and carefully follow all his commands I give you today, the Lord your God will set you high above all the nations on earth. All these blessings will come on you and accompany you if you obey the Lord your God: You will be blessed in the city and blessed in the country."

— Deuteronomy 28:1-3 (NIV)

My Prayer Thoughts

_____

_____

_____

_____

_____

_____

_____

_____

_____

_____

_____

_____

_____

_____

_____

_____

_____

_____

_____

_____

_____

_____

_____

_____

_____

_____

FOR ADDITIONAL STUDY, SEE 2 CORINTHIANS 9:8, PHILIPPIANS 4:19

MY GOOD REPORT

(DEVOTIONAL PAGE 41)

DATE:_____

Hi God –

I have to clear the thoughts of the world out of my head so that I can fill my mind with Your thoughts. You didn't create me to think "low level." That's not how You think! I'm Your child, so I should think like YOU!

HERE ARE SOME OF THE THINGS YOU PROMISE ME:

1. _____

2. _____

3. _____

4. _____

5. _____

Your thoughts are HIGHER than my thoughts. You don't want me to think like the average person, but to think more like You. You want me to think BIG, to dream AMAZING dreams and then go after them. I won't believe dumb thoughts or other people's opinions.

I CAN STRETCH MY FAITH TO BELIEVE YOU FOR:

1. _____

2. _____

3. _____

4. _____

5. _____

I CAN FEEL MY FAITH RISING! WHILE WE'RE TOGETHER, I'D LIKE TO SHARE WITH YOU...

_____

_____

_____

_____

_____

My Prayer Thoughts

_____

_____

_____

_____

_____

_____

_____

_____

_____

_____

_____

_____

_____

For additional study, see Proverbs 23:7, Hebrews 11:1

I CHOOSE YOU

(DEVOTIONAL PAGE 45)

DATE:_____

Hi God –

Attitude is a choice. Joy is a choice. Persistence is a choice. Faith is a choice. Trusting You is a choice. I can either believe in something or NOT. I choose to believe in You! I choose LIFE!

THESE SITUATIONS REQUIRE ME TO CHOOSE A GOOD ATTITUDE, REGARDLESS OF CIRCUMSTANCES:

1. _____

2. _____

3. _____

4. _____

5. _____

If life was a paved path through a rose garden, faith wouldn't be necessary. I have to remember that those things that seem like opposition are actual opportunities because of You. Opportunity for me to grow. Opportunity to advance. Opportunity to take ground. You make all situations work for my benefit, no matter how they look in the natural.

I CHOOSE TO BELIEVE THAT YOU WILL WORK ALL THINGS OUT FOR MY GOOD. HERE ARE SOME OF THE GOOD THINGS I AM BELIEVING YOU FOR:

1. _____

2. _____

3. _____

4. _____

5. _____

I'M ON A FAITH STREAK! I'M BELIEVING FOR BIG THINGS! I WON'T FORGET WHAT YOU'VE ALREADY DONE FOR ME. THANK YOU, FOR...

_____

_____

_____

_____

_____

My Prayer Thoughts

_____

_____

_____

_____

_____

_____

_____

_____

_____

_____

_____

_____

_____

FOR ADDITIONAL STUDY, SEE ROMANS 8:28, JAMES 1:2

I WANT TO COMPLAIN RIGHT NOW

(DEVOTIONAL PAGE 49)

DATE:_____

Hi God –

Complaining about my life doesn't compel You to move…it REPELS You! If I complain, then I'll REMAIN where I am, just like the Israelites.

I REPENT! HERE ARE SOME THINGS I'VE BEEN COMPLAINING ABOUT INSTEAD OF TRUSTING YOU:

1. _____

2. _____

3. _____

4. _____

5. _____

I can let the enemy take my attention away from all that's good and zero in on the one bad thing that's happening right now. But when I do that, I end up being MISERABLE most of the time. Or I can turn it around and be grateful for ALL the good things in my life and trust You with the things that need to change.

I'M GOING TO CHOOSE GRATEFULNESS! THESE ARE THINGS I CAN BE GRATEFUL FOR THIS VERY MOMENT:

1. _____

2. _____

3. _____

4. _____

5. _____

HERE ARE SOME POSITIVE THOUGHTS AND DREAMS THAT I HAVE...

_____

_____

_____

_____

_____

My Prayer Thoughts

_____

_____

_____

_____

_____

_____

_____

_____

_____

_____

_____

_____

_____

FOR ADDITIONAL STUDY, SEE 1 CORINTHIANS 10:10, EPHESIANS 5:20

WHO AM I?

(DEVOTIONAL PAGE 53)

DATE:_____

Hi God –

You're faithful to forgive me and cleanse me of every single thing I've done wrong. You have redeemed me from the shame of my past and my imperfections. I don't have to walk in shame or feel unworthy, because You have forgiven me. And when You forgive, You FORGET! You can't even remember what I did wrong!

I HAVE TO FORGIVE MYSELF! I WILL NOT ALLOW THESE THINGS (IN MY PAST) TO DEFINE ME:

1. _____

2. _____

3. _____

4. _____

5. _____

What I DID is not who I am. Where I LIVE is not who I am. What I DO for a living is not who I am. Who I am is redeemed, forgiven, accepted and made righteous in Christ! What I am is a BLESSING looking for ways to bless someone!

HERE IS WHO YOU SAY I AM:

1. _____

2. _____

3. _____

4. _____

5. _____

NOW THAT I'M WALKING OUT WHO YOU CALLED ME TO BE, I WANT TO SHARE...

_____

_____

_____

_____

_____

My Prayer Thoughts

• • ● ● ● • •

I DON'T KNOW WHAT TO SAY

(DEVOTIONAL PAGE 57)

DATE:_____

Hi God –

I will remember all of the good things You've done for me so far. I will talk about the time You brought unexpected money into my life, just when I needed it most. I'll remember the time You healed me of the headache, the cold, the backache and so much more. I will say, out loud, to the universe how GOOD You've been to me, how You saved me, how You redeemed me, how You keep lifting me up even when I fail and fall short.

RIGHT NOW, I RECORD AND READ OUT LOUD TO THE WORLD, I REMEMBER THE TIME THAT GOD:

1. _____

2. _____

3. _____

4. _____

5. _____

And now, I speak to the problem. You have a limited shelf life and I have been given authority, in the name of Jesus, to pull you out of my life. I put you in your place, under my feet, where you won't hurt anyone ever again! So GET OUT of my life; be quieted, be stilled, be stopped and removed! I refuse to allow you any power in my life. That's my God's place!

SO, RIGHT NOW, I COMMAND THIS SITUATION TO:

1. _____

2. _____

3. _____

4. _____

5. _____

Father, You say that whatever I ask for, in the name of Jesus, You will do for me. So I ask You, right now, to remove the problem, never to be seen by me again. Problem, you will not come back a second time!

I'M SO GLAD YOU'RE HERE FOR ME TO TALK TO. I WANT TO TELL YOU...

_____

_____

_____

My Prayer Thoughts

_____

_____

_____

_____

_____

_____

_____

_____

_____

_____

_____

_____

_____

FOR ADDITIONAL STUDY, SEE 2 CORINTHIANS 4:13, JOSHUA 1:8

· • ● **●** ● • ·

I WON'T QUIT

(DEVOTIONAL PAGE 61)

DATE:_____

Hi God –

I'm not alone! You promise to NEVER leave me, no matter where I go. You're with me all the time, because You're just that GOOD! You're a friend who sticks closer than any brother ever would. Nothing ever takes You by surprise.

HERE ARE SOME THINGS YOU'RE WALKING ME THROUGH:

1. _____

2. _____

3. _____

4. _____

5. _____

Why would I ever feel like quitting if I have You with me? I know You're ALWAYS with me. You surround me at all times. If You equip me—and You have, if You give me strength—and You do, if You fight for me—and You have, as promised, why would I EVER quit?

I WON'T QUIT! INSTEAD, I WILL:

1. _____

2. _____

3. _____

4. _____

5. _____

I FEEL YOU'RE PROMPTING ME TO...

_____

_____

_____

_____

_____

My Prayer Thoughts

_____

_____

_____

_____

_____

_____

_____

_____

_____

_____

_____

_____

_____

FOR ADDITIONAL STUDY, SEE GENESIS 28:15, NEHEMIAH 8:10

NO DOUBT

(DEVOTIONAL PAGE 65)

DATE:_____

Hi God –

The enemy tries to make me doubt who I am and why You'd ever do anything for me. (Mostly so I won't even ask You.) He does that because he knows Your power. It's time I believe in Your power at LEAST as much as the devil does!

HERE ARE SOME DOUBTS THAT THE ENEMY IS THROWING AT ME:

1. _____

2. _____

3. _____

4. _____

5. _____

But I can ask in faith, no wavering, no doubting…just BELIEVING! I believe that You are great! I believe that You love me beyond what

I can even understand. I believe that Jesus died so that I can live. I can't earn anything…it's a FREE GIFT. You just love me that much!

I AM THE BELIEVER. YOU ARE THE PERFORMER. I WILL ASK IN FAITH. NO DOUBTING. FATHER, RIGHT NOW I ASK YOU FOR…

1. _____

2. _____

3. _____

4. _____

5. _____

I'M SO THANKFUL FOR YOUR GRACE! I JUST WANTED TO TELL YOU…

_____

_____

_____

_____

_____

My Prayer Thoughts

FOR ADDITIONAL STUDY, SEE GENESIS 3:1-5, MATTHEW 4:1-11

• • ● • •

LAUGHTER, NOT WORRY

(DEVOTIONAL PAGE 69)

DATE:_____

Hi God –

You said to give You all my worries, the stuff that's weighing me down and the things that keep me awake at night. You care for me. You're well able to carry it. You WANT me to trust You enough to give it ALL to You. I do trust You.

JUST SOME OF THE THINGS I'VE WORRIED ABOUT AND NEED TO GIVE TO YOU ARE:

1. _____

2. _____

3. _____

4. _____

5. _____

By deciding to trust You with my cares, I can make the decision, right now, that I'm going to be HAPPY and enjoy the day. I feel the way I feel because I think the way I think. As a man thinks, so he is.

I WILL PURPOSEFULLY THINK ABOUT GOOD THINGS TODAY, THINGS LIKE:

1. _____

2. _____

3. _____

4. _____

5. _____

ALSO, I JUST WANT TO TELL YOU...

_____

_____

_____

I'm giving my cares, concerns and worries to You, right now, and releasing them! Because You are ABLE to do so much more than I can ask, think, imagine or even dream. You've already solved problems I haven't even thought of yet!

My Prayer Thoughts

_____

_____

_____

_____

_____

_____

_____

_____

_____

_____

_____

_____

_____

For additional study, see 2 Corinthians 10:5, Romans 12:2

I CRY OUT TO YOU

(DEVOTIONAL PAGE 73)

DATE:_____

Hi God –

I've been messing up! I've been putting more faith in the junk and the people who are bothering me than in You and Your ability to handle it. I can't fix people. I can't fix the problem. But You can! Nothing is too big for You!!! Instead of crying, I'll cry out TO You. Your promise says that when my heart is broken and I feel crushed, and I cry out to You, You'll save me from all that's hurting me.

RIGHT NOW, I CRY OUT IN FAITH AND INVITE YOU TO HELP WITH:

1. _____

2. _____

3. _____

4. _____

5. _____

Now my time isn't wasted; it's productive. Time with You makes me strong. It dries my tears. It restores my soul. I don't end up spent. I end up loosing the power of the Mighty God on my behalf. With You on my side, who or what can mess with me?

I REMEMBER WHEN YOU HELPED ME BEFORE.
I REMEMBER WHEN:

1. _____

2. _____

3. _____

4. _____

5. _____

I have the best security, most awesome healer, seer of the future, and lover of my soul working on my behalf. That gives me strength! It isn't me; it's YOU! You're the only One who can handle this. I was trying to do it all by myself.

WHILE I AM WITH YOU, I CAN'T FORGET TO TELL YOU...

_____

_____

_____

My Prayer Thoughts

_____

_____

_____

_____

_____

_____

_____

_____

_____

_____

_____

_____

_____

FOR ADDITIONAL STUDY, SEE PSALMS 34:6, 17-18, ISAIAH 40:31, ROMANS 8:31

ENEMY WHO?

(DEVOTIONAL PAGE 77)

DATE:_____

Hi God –

You didn't say that TROUBLE would never come my way. Or that I wouldn't have any enemies. You said that I have nothing to fear. Love never fails. My job is to walk in love while You fight my battles. You give me victories I could only dream of. When trouble tries to rear its ugly head, You have my back, and peace is headed my way.

FATHER, HELP ME WALK IN LOVE WITH THESE PEOPLE:

1. _____

2. _____

3. _____

4. _____

5. _____

Consciously, I put my trust in You. I will do what You say. And when my ways please You, You MAKE my enemies be at peace with me. And, God, I know You know how to MAKE things happen! BOOM!

HERE ARE SOME OF MY WAYS THAT YOU WANT ME TO WORK ON AND CHANGE:

1. _____

2. _____

3. _____

4. _____

5. _____

My enemies, whether it's a problem or a situation, don't stand a chance with You on my side. I'm not only a winner, I'm MORE than a conqueror, through You. You love me!

I JUST WANTED TO TELL YOU...

_____

_____

_____

_____

_____

My Prayer Thoughts

_____

_____

_____

_____

_____

_____

_____

_____

_____

_____

_____

_____

_____

_____

_____

_____

_____

_____

_____

_____

_____

_____

_____

_____

_____

_____

_____

_____

_____

For additional study, see Proverbs 16:7, Romans 8:37

STEPPING OUT

(DEVOTIONAL PAGE 81)

DATE:_____

Hi God –

If I walk by sight, the situation I see with my eyes won't allow me to step out of the boat and try to walk on water. But JESUS told Peter to "come." Where You lead me, it's my job to follow. You want to purposely lead me to places that require faith. I don't have to see it to believe it. You want me to believe in what I can't see! That PROVES that I have faith in You and what You're doing.

I CAN TELL THAT YOU ARE WANTING ME TO STRETCH MY FAITH IN THE AREAS OF:

1. _____

2. _____

3. _____

4. _____

5. _____

You say that You do things for me according to my faith. That's why You want me to have faith, so that You can move on my behalf! I believe that You are able!

I BELIEVE BY FAITH THAT YOU WILL:

1. _____

2. _____

3. _____

4. _____

5. _____

I WANTED TO SHARE FROM MY HEART WITH YOU ABOUT...

_____

_____

_____

_____

You don't ask me to believe for the possible. (I could probably do that alone.) You want me to believe for the impossible, because that takes trusting You. I give You all the glory! With me, it's impossible. But it's not me; it's YOU!

My Prayer Thoughts

FOR ADDITIONAL STUDY, SEE PROVERBS 16:7, ROMANS 8:37

HURRY UP!

(DEVOTIONAL PAGE 85)

DATE:_____

Hi God –

I don't have to be afraid. You're with me! Your strength and courage lead and guide me on the right path at the right time. You're always stretching my dreams and enlarging my possibilities. You have MORE for me!

It has to be big enough that I can't do it without You! I won't hold back. I can do this. I can dream with the God of the universe! Here I go!

I TAKE THE LIBERTY TO DREAM BIG RIGHT NOW.
I DREAM THAT:

1. _____

2. _____

3. _____

4. _____

5. _____

You're taking me on this fantastic trip, one small step at a time. I want it now, but You seem to know just how much I can take at once. You want me to live in Your land of promise. Little by little I can do this, with You! Inch by inch, it will be a cinch!

HERE ARE TRAITS I BELIEVE YOU WILL GROW AND IMPROVE IN ME:

1. _____

2. _____

3. _____

4. _____

5. _____

THANK YOU FOR BELIEVING IN ME. I WANTED TO TALK WITH YOU ABOUT...

_____

_____

_____

My Prayer Thoughts

_____

_____

_____

_____

_____

_____

_____

_____

_____

_____

_____

_____

_____

_____

BEING ME

(DEVOTIONAL PAGE 89)

DATE:_____

Hi God –

I am not living a random existence or ordinary life. You had ME precisely in mind from the very beginning. You not only formed me with all my quirkiness, freckles, and interesting ways, You gave me this unique personality that I sometimes question. You CALLED me by my name. You had me, my name and my life in Your mind.

SOME OF THE UNIQUE, CURIOUS AND INTERESTING TRAITS I HAVE ARE:

1. _____

2. _____

3. _____

4. _____

5. _____

God, thank You that You aren't waiting for me to be perfect to use me. If that were the case, You would never have anyone to use! You have a great purpose and exciting plans for me. I have a hope-filled, prosperous, purpose-filled future. I know You'll use me to help people in a way no one else could.

No one can be a better ME than me. I am the only me You created, and anyone else trying to be me could never pull it off!

HERE ARE SEVERAL WAYS I CAN USE THESE SPECIAL TRAITS TO MAKE A DIFFERENCE FOR YOU:

1. _____

2. _____

3. _____

4. _____

5. _____

I JUST WANTED TO TAKE A MOMENT TO SHARE...

_____

_____

_____

My Prayer Thoughts

_____

_____

_____

_____

_____

_____

_____

_____

_____

_____

_____

_____

_____

_____

FOR ADDITIONAL STUDY, SEE ISAIAH 43:7, JEREMIAH 29:11, PSALM 119:73-74

• • ● ● ● • •

FEAR NOT

(DEVOTIONAL PAGE 93)

DATE:_____

Hi God –

Fear and faith have something in common. They BOTH ask me to believe in something I can't see. So I choose to believe in You. I will believe in You more than I believe in the things that scare me.

THE ENEMY HAS TRIED TO GET ME TO FEAR IN THESE AREAS:

1. _____

2. _____

3. _____

4. _____

5. _____

When I operate in fear and try to make decisions, I'm functioning at a LOW intellectual state. Fear tolerated is faith contaminated. I don't have to be afraid. You're with me. You have what it takes to protect me and keep me safe. I will make faith-filled decisions with Your help.

THESE ARE SOME SCARY DECISIONS I NEED TO MAKE IN FAITH:

1. _____

2. _____

3. _____

4. _____

5. _____

THANK YOU FOR BEING WITH ME AND LISTENING AS I PRAY ABOUT...

_____

_____

_____

You custom designed my future and my dreams for me. Not for someone else, but for me! That's why I have to PUSH PAST my fears and achieve the dreams and the destiny You've created for me. Life's not about fearing; it's about fulfilling. I will do it, even if I am afraid.

My Prayer Thoughts

_____

_____

_____

_____

_____

_____

_____

_____

_____

_____

_____

_____

_____

_____

_____

_____

_____

_____

_____

_____

_____

_____

_____

_____

_____

_____

_____

FOR ADDITIONAL STUDY, SEE PSALM 23:4, ROMANS 1:17 AMP

• • ● • •

MORE THAN ENOUGH

(DEVOTIONAL PAGE 97)

DATE:_____

Hi God –

There are areas of my life that are just lacking. I know my mind goes immediately to dollar signs. But there are other areas of my life that I need You to touch as well. You're generous with me in EVERY capacity that I need as long as I'm generous with You and obey Your instructions.

HERE ARE PARTS OF MY LIFE THAT I'M GOING TO TURN OVER TO YOU, MY MORE-THAN-ENOUGH GOD:

1. _____

2. _____

3. _____

4. _____

5. _____

You ask me to give, but no matter what, I can't out-give You. But I can OBEY You. And I can and do stand on the promises from You! Thank You, God!

I will GIVE in the way You ask me to. You promise to hold the enemy back from taking what I have, from hurting what is mine and stealing of my time by requiring repairs and resources. You don't just hold the enemy back, You rebuke him for me!

You promise that when I am generous to You, it comes back to me SO many times more than what I gave. Your blessing is pushed down, shaken together, trying to fit more into one blessing but it STILL overflows!

THESE ARE SOME WAYS I WOULD LIKE TO BE MORE GENEROUS:

1. _____

2. _____

3. _____

WHILE WE ARE TALKING ABOUT GIVING, I WANT TO SHARE...

1. _____

2. _____

3. _____

My Prayer Thoughts

_____

_____

_____

_____

_____

_____

_____

_____

_____

_____

_____

_____

For additional study, see Isaiah 48:17, Malachi 3:11, Luke 6:38

IT HURTS TO FORGIVE

(DEVOTIONAL PAGE 101)

DATE:_____

Hi God –

With the help of Your grace, I CHOOSE to forgive all those who have wronged me in any way. As I forgive, I'm unburdened by the mistakes of others and I have peace in my mind. I choose not to be offended. I choose to let it go. I choose to put it in Your capable hands. I choose to be a great forgiver. I choose to live in freedom!

BY FAITH, I CHOOSE TO FORGIVE THESE THINGS:

1. _____

2. _____

3. _____

4. _____

5. _____

When I forgive, I disappoint the devil! I short-circuit his plan to steal my blessing, my joy and my peace. Today, God, I disappoint the devil and I please YOU! I take a massive step toward Your plan of blessing and freedom for my life!

AS I GIVE FORGIVENESS TO OTHERS, I ASK YOUR FORGIVENESS FOR:

1. _____

2. _____

3. _____

4. _____

5. _____

THANK YOU FOR BEING WITH ME AND LISTENING AS I PRAY ABOUT...

_____

_____

_____

I choose to let Your grace and love work in me and through me. I choose to live healthier and happier by forgiving, being forgiven and trusting You. I choose to turn past disappointment into my divine appointment.

My Prayer Thoughts

_____

_____

_____

_____

_____

_____

_____

_____

_____

_____

_____

_____

_____

_____

_____

_____

_____

_____

_____

_____

_____

_____

_____

_____

_____

FOR ADDITIONAL STUDY, SEE EPHESIANS 4:27, 31-32, 2 CORINTHIANS 2:10-11

• • ● ● ● • •

IN NEED OF COMPANIONSHIP

(DEVOTIONAL PAGE 105)

DATE:_____

Hi God —

I've heard it said, "Show me your friends, and I'll show you your future." Whoever walks with wise friends becomes WISE. I will not choose relationships with people who are not good for me just because I'm lonely or it's convenient.

THESE ARE THE TYPES OF PEOPLE I SHOULD HANG AROUND WITH:

1. _____

2. _____

3. _____

4. _____

5. _____

I will choose GODLY friends. I will have relationships that will foster success and help me stay on track, according to the purpose that You have for me. I won't develop bonds with people who just happen to be nearby, who might drag me down or out of my purpose. I will wait for the right people who You are sending into my life.

I SHOULD INVEST MORE TIME AND ENERGY AND DEVELOP A BETTER RELATIONSHIP WITH:

1. _____

2. _____

3. _____

4. _____

5. _____

THE BEST RELATIONSHIP I CAN HAVE IS WITH YOU. I'VE BEEN WANTING TO TELL YOU ABOUT...

_____

_____

_____

_____

My Prayer Thoughts

_____

_____

_____

_____

_____

_____

_____

_____

_____

_____

_____

_____

_____

FOR ADDITIONAL STUDY, SEE PROVERBS 12:26, 13:20, 27:17

A NEW NAME

(DEVOTIONAL PAGE 109)

DATE:_____

Hi God –

Even though I don't often feel like a winner or a priceless treasure, You see me that way and You call me by that name. And Your Word doesn't come back to You without accomplishing what You sent it to do!

HERE ARE SOME OLD NAMES THAT I'VE BEEN CALLING MYSELF:

1. _____

2. _____

3. _____

4. _____

5. _____

No more of this "I'm just a..." talk. You have forgotten my past. You don't dwell on my present. You push me toward my future. It's clear to You, and You're trying to make it clear to me! I don't have to do this alone. I don't have to become something on my own. I can do this—with You!

Even if I'm shy about believing everything You've called me to be, I can latch onto the fact that You will HELP ME be those things!

YOU ARE IN ME, SO I CAN BELIEVE THESE GOOD THINGS ABOUT MYSELF:

1. _____

2. _____

3. _____

4. _____

5. _____

WITH YOUR ENCOURAGEMENT IN MY HEART, I WANT TO SAY...

_____

_____

_____

My Prayer Thoughts

_____

_____

_____

_____

_____

_____

_____

_____

_____

_____

_____

_____

_____

_____

FOR ADDITIONAL STUDY, SEE EPHESIANS 2:10, REVELATION 12:11, DEUTERONOMY 28:1-14

I WANT TO BE HAPPY

(DEVOTIONAL PAGE 113)

DATE:_____

Hi God –

You promise that ALL things work together for my good. (Even the stinky moments, days or weeks.) The enemy is trying to wreck my happiness and peace. But You made a PROMISE. No matter what happens, even if someone intentionally tries to hurt me, You will use it for my own good.

THESE THINGS ARE TRYING TO STEAL MY "HAPPY," BUT I COUNT THEM ALL AS JOY!

1. _____

2. _____

3. _____

4. _____

5. _____

Joy isn't what happens TO me; it is what happens THROUGH me! You are in me trying to come out. In those moments, I will trust that You have something good planned for me beyond what I can see right now.

HERE ARE SOME GOOD THINGS THAT I SEE HAPPENING BY FAITH:

1. _____

2. _____

3. _____

4. _____

5. _____

I WANT TO SHARE...

_____

_____

_____

_____

_____

My Prayer Thoughts

_____

_____

_____

_____

_____

_____

_____

_____

_____

_____

_____

_____

_____

FOR ADDITIONAL STUDY, SEE ROMANS 8:28, GENESIS 50:20

WHAT'S GOOD ABOUT ME?

(DEVOTIONAL PAGE 117)

DATE:_____

Hi God –

My power doesn't come from me; it comes from YOU. You live inside me. You're greater than I can ever dream of being. You're here inside of me waiting to come out! I have to listen to You and not to the enemy, the inner me, or to those trying to put me down. I will purpose in my soul to listen to You!

THERE ARE ATTRIBUTES THAT YOU WANT TO SHINE OUT THROUGH ME. SOME OF THEM ARE:

1. _____

2. _____

3. _____

4. _____

5. _____

You don't create junk. You created me and put me on this planet to do good. Because of You, no matter what I think, I am GOOD! I pray that my eyes are enlightened; that I see in myself what You see in me. It wells up on the inside of me. I will use it. I will increase my natural strengths. I will use my gifts for You and to help other people.

HERE ARE SOME GIFTS AND TALENTS YOU'VE GIVEN ME THAT MAKE ME SPECIAL:

1. _____

2. _____

3. _____

4. _____

WHEN I THINK ABOUT THE GOOD YOU SEE IN ME, I WANT TO SAY...

_____

_____

_____

I vow that I will listen to You and lean into You more. I will tune into Your voice. I will live and fulfill the intended purpose that You designed for me. Your future for me looks great!

My Prayer Thoughts

_____

_____

_____

_____

_____

_____

_____

_____

_____

_____

_____

_____

For additional study, see 1 John 4:4, Proverbs 2:2, 4:20, Ephesians 2:10

HEAL ME!

(DEVOTIONAL PAGE 121)

DATE:_____

Hi God –

Jesus Christ bore my grief, my sorrow, my sickness and my pain on the cross. He has redeemed me from the curse of the law. If He died for me to live free (and He did), then there is no place in my body for sickness or pain. For God sent His Word and I AM healed. I receive that gift and live healed.

I LIVE HEALED BECAUSE I DECLARE THESE SYSTEMS OF MY BODY TO FUNCTION PROPERLY:

1. _____

2. _____

3. _____

4. _____

5. _____

You created me in Your image. I am beautifully and wonderfully made. Sickness and disease have NO PLACE in my body. They are trespassers and I declare they are in my body illegally. Therefore, I say, "Get out of my body, in Jesus' name! You have no right to be here!"

I DON'T JUST SPEAK TO THE PROBLEM; I HAVE FAITH FOR THE SOLUTION. THESE PARTS OF MY BODY ARE HEALED, IN JESUS' NAME.

1. _____

2. _____

3. _____

4. _____

5. _____

I IMAGINE ALL THE THINGS I'M GOING TO DO WHEN MY HEALING STARTS TO MANIFEST!

_____

_____

_____

_____

My Prayer Thoughts

_____

_____

_____

_____

_____

_____

_____

_____

_____

_____

_____

_____

_____

_____

For additional study, see Genesis 1:27, Psalm 139:13-14

WHEN PEOPLE HURT ME

(DEVOTIONAL PAGE 125)

DATE:_____

Hi God –

After they beat Him with whips, pulled the beard out of His face and crucified Him, Jesus hung on the cross. He said, "FORGIVE them, because they know not what they're doing." If Jesus can forgive all that, then surely I can give grace to the people who hurt my feelings.

SHOW ME HOW TO FORGIVE THESE PEOPLE WHO HURT ME:

1. _____

2. _____

3. _____

4. _____

5. _____

I won't hold back. I'm tempted to quit giving so much of myself and getting hurt...but I won't. I won't build a wall around my heart to keep people out. The enemy would sure like that. He wants me to think that I'm all alone against the world. NO! That would only hurt me!

Only You, God, can turn a hurt into a benefit. I believe that You have people seeking me out right now for friendship and relationship, for fun and love and for good times and laughs. I believe You have someone praying to meet someone just like ME, the same way I am praying for a new relationship right now.

I WILL BE OPEN TO NEW RELATIONSHIPS AND TO ALLOW NEW FRIENDSHIPS TO FORM BY:

1. _____

2. _____

3. _____

Thank You, God, for being with me when I feel betrayed and HURT. Thank You for holding me up when I want to quit. Thank You for being one step ahead of me, preparing someone's heart to be a confidant and a dear friend to me.

AND WHILE WE'RE TALKING...

_____

_____

My Prayer Thoughts

_____

_____

_____

_____

_____

_____

_____

_____

_____

_____

_____

_____

_____

_____

_____

_____

_____

_____

_____

_____

_____

_____

_____

_____

_____

For additional study, see Luke 23:34, 2 Corinthians 12:9

WHAT I DO MATTERS

(DEVOTIONAL PAGE 129)

DATE:_____

Hi God –

You planned for me to be alive for this moment in time, for a purpose that I might not know yet. But, You know. You don't waste Your time on random acts. You know the end from the beginning. Everything You do is on purpose, and that means I am ON PURPOSE. I am planned, intended, needed and significant. This means that I matter.

HERE ARE SOME THINGS IN MY LIFE THAT SEEM RANDOM AND UNEXPLAINABLE:

1. _____

2. _____

3. _____

4. _____

5. _____

You, God, King of kings and Lord of lords, took time to create me! You only do things that matter. You spent Your valuable time thinking exactly how You would construct me, just the way I am, right here in this particular year, in this city at this job, with this EXACT personality. I am gifted in my own quirky way. I say quirky but You say I'm a masterpiece!

HERE ARE SOME WAYS I BELIEVE YOU COULD PUT MY UNIQUE TRAITS AND TALENTS TO WORK FOR YOU:

1. _____

2. _____

3. _____

4. _____

5. _____

You have a destiny and purpose for ME—little ol' me, created intentionally me, needed by God for a purpose me, intended and destined by the Creator and Child of the King me!

I WANT TO DREAM FOR A MINUTE ABOUT THINGS I CAN DO FOR YOU THAT WILL REALLY MATTER...

_____

_____

_____

My Prayer Thoughts

_____

_____

_____

_____

_____

_____

_____

_____

_____

_____

_____

_____

_____

FOR ADDITIONAL STUDY, SEE EPHESIANS 2:10, GALATIANS 2:20

I FEEL UNLOVED

(DEVOTIONAL PAGE 133)

DATE:_____

Hi God –

When people do me wrong, I get mad or offended, and then I write people off. I'm so glad that You're not like me. You don't stop loving me when I fail. You NEVER do. No matter what I do, You're not going to consider me a hopeless case! Your Word says that right this very minute, Jesus Himself is praying for me at Your right hand. You wouldn't pray for me if You didn't love me. All this time, I've been looking for a "feeling" instead of realizing that there is proof right here in black and white.

HERE ARE SOME TIMES WHEN I THOUGHT YOU MIGHT GIVE UP ON ME...BUT YOU LOVED ME ANYWAY:

1. _____

2. _____

3. _____

4. _____

5. _____

Your love for me is so beyond my comprehension. YOU KNEW what I would do wrong before I was even born. And still You sent Jesus to the cross to die for me, 2,000 years before I existed. You love me NO MATTER WHAT, and I thank You today! Thank You for loving me. Thank You for believing in me enough to create me, even though You knew my mess. Thank You for never giving up on me.

HERE ARE SOME WAYS THAT YOU MAKE ME FEEL LOVED:

1. _____

2. _____

3. _____

4. _____

5. _____

I WANT TO LOVE LIKE YOU. LOVE SHARES, SO I WANT TO SHARE WITH YOU...

_____

_____

_____

My Prayer Thoughts

_____

_____

_____

_____

_____

_____

_____

_____

_____

_____

_____

_____

For additional study, see Genesis 28:15, Romans 5:8

I WON'T HOLD BACK

(DEVOTIONAL PAGE 137)

DATE:_____

Hi God –

I'm not going to let the enemy dwarf my future any longer by being too timid to ASK You for stuff. You're waiting for me to believe that You're bigger than I can ever imagine. You're wanting me to trust You at a level that I can't accomplish myself. You desire that my faith in You exceeds my capacity to accomplish things on my own.

YOU WANT ME TO TRUST YOU WITH BIG THINGS, THINGS LIKE:

1. _____

2. _____

3. _____

4. _____

5. _____

I am strong in the Lord and the power of His might. I am strong in You. I can ask BIG things through You. I will believe in You even more! Today, God, I take You at Your Word and I ask You for what I need! Right this moment, I grab hold of Your Promises...and I will not let go!

Today, I am going to have audacious faith, bold faith, believe-God-is-bigger-than-I-can-even-imagine faith!

RIGHT NOW, GOD, I ASK YOU FOR:

1. _____

2. _____

3. _____

4. _____

5. _____

THANK YOU FOR TELLING ME TO ASK. I AM GROWING IN MY TRUST IN YOU. AND WHILE I'M SHARING THINGS WITH YOU...

_____

_____

_____

My Prayer Thoughts

_____

_____

_____

_____

_____

_____

_____

_____

_____

_____

_____

_____

_____

FOR ADDITIONAL STUDY, SEE MATTHEW 7:7, 21:22, PROVERBS 3:5-6

• • ● ● ● • •

I'M ALL WORKED UP

(DEVOTIONAL PAGE 141)

DATE:_____

Hi God –

I got mad and started handling business without stopping to ask for Your direction, grace or wisdom. And now…I sure do need You!

God, right now I apologize for acting without You. I repent for thinking I could handle the aggravations of life on my own. I don't want these CARES. I want You! I give these problems to You right now and ask You for the wisdom, guidance and direction to make the right decisions. Lord, I trust You. I know You have me in the palm of Your hand.

HERE ARE SOME SITUATIONS WHERE I KIND OF WENT OFF THE DEEP END:

1. _____

2. _____

3. _____

4. _____

5. _____

I haven't earned it and I don't deserve it, but You're still willing to help me with my problems. When I reach out to You and listen for Your voice, You give me the WISDOM to solve my problems in return.

You whisper in my ear about what to do and when to do it. You lead me out of trouble and into Your blessing!

I'M LISTENING TO YOU, GOD, AND I THINK YOU WOULD BE PLEASED IF I:

1. _____

2. _____

3. _____

4. _____

5. _____

WHILE I AM TALKING TO YOU...

_____

_____

_____

My Prayer Thoughts

_____

_____

_____

_____

_____

_____

_____

_____

_____

_____

_____

_____

_____

_____

FOR ADDITIONAL STUDY, SEE 1 JOHN 3:20, PSALM 37:5, ISAIAH 49:16

WHEN I NEED TO SAY NO

(DEVOTIONAL PAGE 145)

DATE:_____

Hi God –

"No" can be a great word. It can keep me from wasting my time and energy. It can guide ME toward the doors that You have for me. When I have trouble saying NO to people, instead of answering right then, I will respond with, *"I'll pray about it."*

You've just been waiting for me to look to You for my next step. Here are some situations where I need Your guidance.

SHOULD I SAY YES OR SHOULD I SAY NO?

1. _____

2. _____

3. _____

4. _____

5. _____

I have always wanted to know my purpose. Your Word says that my purpose is to please God, not people. You examine the motives of my heart and determine how You can bless me. You're the one who promotes me...NOT my boss. You lift me up.

With prayer, I will have the courage to say "no" to temptations, tasks, events and relationships that are not in Your perfect will for me. That leaves room for me to say "yes" to You. Thank You for the knowledge, understanding, and courage to walk into Your BEST yes for me!

HERE ARE SOME THINGS I'VE GOTTEN MYSELF INTO IN THE PAST THAT DIDN'T TURN OUT SO WELL:

1. _____

2. _____

3. _____

4. _____

AS I'M PRAYING ABOUT HOW TO GET FROM PLEASING PEOPLE, TO PLEASING YOU...

_____

_____

My Prayer Thoughts

_____

_____

_____

_____

_____

_____

_____

_____

_____

_____

_____

_____

_____

For additional study, see Colossians 3:15, Romans 12:2, Psalm 37:23

WHAT AM I LOOKING AT?

(DEVOTIONAL PAGE 149)

DATE:_____

Hi God –

When it looks bad and I'm surrounded by, overwhelmed with, and in the very presence of enemies, that's actually an opportunity for You to SHOW OUT! I won't look at the enemy. I will look to You!

With Your help, it doesn't matter who is coming at me! With You on my side, my enemies don't stand a chance. They'll fall like David's giant. They'll be defeated like Joshua's mountain land. They'll be swallowed up like the army that came after Moses.

IT LOOKS LIKE THESE ENEMIES ARE COMING AFTER ME TODAY:

1. _____

2. _____

3. _____

4. _____

5. _____

You want my enemies to see that You are FOR me. You want the world to note that what happened was impossible. You want to set the stage, set the table, and set the circumstances right in front of my enemies for Your miracle to be noted. Set the table, God!

I might not have started this fight, but as I turn my eyes off of the fight and look at You, I know this: My God is going to finish it! BOOM!!!

I TAKE THE LIMITS OFF OF MY MIRACLE-WORKING GOD. HERE'S HOW YOU WILL MAKE MY ENEMIES PAY:

1. _____

2. _____

3. _____

4. _____

THANK YOU FOR BEING BIGGER THAN I CAN ASK, THINK OR IMAGINE. WHILE MY FAITH IS HIGH, I WOULD LIKE TO SAY...

_____

_____

_____

My Prayer Thoughts

_____

_____

_____

_____

_____

_____

_____

_____

_____

_____

_____

_____

_____

For additional study, see Psalm 18:29, 2 Corinthians 4:18

A PEARL OF GREAT PRICE

(DEVOTIONAL PAGE 153)

DATE:_____

Hi God –

Jesus literally gave His all for me. He gave His life, His death and His suffering. He willingly took my pain, my sin, my problems, my shortcomings and my embarrassments. Then He gave EVERYTHING He had. He gave it all for me…and I wasn't even born yet.

Jesus, I am so grateful for Your sacrifice. If You died for it, I don't have to live with it.

HERE ARE SOME THINGS THAT I DON'T HAVE TO LIVE WITH ANYMORE:

1. _____

2. _____

3. _____

4. _____

5. _____

I didn't pick me. You picked me. You thought about me and created me. You have a plan for me. You have a purpose for me. You're in heaven praying for me. You're believing in ME!

Thank You, God, for loving me SO much that Your Son died for me. Right now, I ask You for the confidence to move forward into the bright future that You have for me. How do I know my future is brighter than I can imagine? Because Your Word says so!!!

WITH YOU IN CONTROL OF MY LIFE, I CAN DARE TO IMAGINE:

1. _____

2. _____

3. _____

4. _____

SINCE YOU ALREADY KNOW EVERYTHING I'VE DONE AND PAID THE PRICE FOR IT, I FEEL BETTER TELLING YOU...

_____

_____

_____

My Prayer Thoughts

FOR ADDITIONAL STUDY, SEE ROMANS 3:23, JOHN 3:16

I GOTTA LOVE WHO?

(DEVOTIONAL PAGE 157)

DATE:_____

Hi God –

You say whatever I sow, I will reap. I want LOVE in my life. I need forgiveness for the things I admit and things I don't want to admit. So to get forgiveness in my life, I need to give it away. Some things are easy to give. Others are much harder.

I NEED FORGIVENESS FROM YOU. BUT I ALSO NEED TO FORGIVE MYSELF FOR :

1. _____

2. _____

3. _____

4. _____

5. _____

I want Your love when I don't DESERVE it. So I will give love to those who don't deserve it. I want Your forgiveness when I have no excuse for my action. So I will forgive people who have no excuse for their actions.

At first, this might all be by faith. I might need to come to You for the strength to do it, every single day. I might, occasionally, need to ask You to forgive me for stepping out of love. But that's the beauty of You. You'll forgive me AGAIN and again and always love me.

As Your child, I have to follow in my Father's footsteps and love the people who I can't love on my own. It will take Your power and forgiveness in me.

RIGHT NOW, I NEED YOUR HELP FORGIVING AND LOVING THESE PEOPLE:

1. _____

2. _____

3. _____

4. _____

5. _____

My Prayer Thoughts

_____

_____

_____

_____

_____

_____

_____

_____

_____

_____

_____

_____

FOR ADDITIONAL STUDY, SEE MATTHEW 6:14, 18:21-22

WHAT SHOULD I DO?

(DEVOTIONAL PAGE 161)

DATE:_____

Hi God –

You tell me in Your Word that I only see through a glass darkly and that my eyes don't really see what they need to see. I need to LEAN IN to You. But still, I have to fight to balance on my own.

I do lean...like on a balance beam. If I lean too far in one direction, that's the way I'm going to fall. Why shouldn't I fall into Your arms, into Your GRACE, Your mercy and Your wisdom? You always take care of me. I just need to trust You more, instead of trusting my own mind.

I NEED TO LEAN ON YOU MORE IN THESE AREAS:

1. _____

2. _____

3. _____

4. _____

5. _____

I lean on Your promise to guide me, to teach me, to direct me in the way I should go. I rely on You to show me what is right and to reveal to me what is BEST.

God, I invite You to lead me through this. My peace will be the indicator of which way I should go. Even if my head doesn't understand, I will let my heart trust in You to guide and direct me in all that I do.

SO I AM ASKING YOU TO LEAD ME. I'M SO EXCITED TO SEE WHAT YOU HAVE FOR ME. THESE ARE SOME NEW AREAS THAT I'M REALLY LOOKING FORWARD TO:

1. _____

2. _____

3. _____

4. _____

WHILE I'M LEANING ON YOU, I NEED TO TALK TO YOU ABOUT...

_____

_____

_____

My Prayer Thoughts

_____

_____

_____

_____

_____

_____

_____

_____

_____

_____

_____

_____

_____

_____

_____

_____

_____

_____

_____

_____

_____

_____

_____

_____

_____

_____

_____

_____

For additional study, see 1 Corinthians 13:12, Matthew 21:22

I'M FEELING MOODY

(DEVOTIONAL PAGE 165)

DATE:_____

Hi God –

Whatever just blew up in my life and tried to ruin my mood is just an opportunity for You to show me how You can make things beautiful again. You promise to give me beauty for ashes. If I doubt that promise, that wouldn't please You. You can put HAPPINESS in my heart when I look past the problem and look directly at You.

You say to count it ALL joy. If I can't count it as joy, I'm thinking about the wrong things.

SOME OF THE WRONG THINGS I'VE BEEN THINKING ABOUT ARE:

1. _____

2. _____

3. _____

4. _____

5. _____

Forgive me, Father, for forgetting the benefits of being Your baby: forgiveness, healing, Your love, Your kindness and Your favor. Having FAVOR from You that I didn't earn, now that's something that changes any mood! Thank You, Lord! So, what do I need to think about in order to change the way I feel? You say that I should think about the things in my life that are GOOD, HAPPY and LOVELY!

WHAT IS THERE THAT I CAN BE THANKFUL FOR?

1. _____

2. _____

3. _____

4. _____

5. _____

AS LONG AS I'M BEING PURPOSEFUL ABOUT CHANGING MY MOOD, I WANT TO TELL YOU ABOUT...

_____

_____

_____

My Prayer Thoughts

_____

_____

_____

_____

_____

_____

_____

_____

_____

_____

_____

_____

_____

FOR ADDITIONAL STUDY, SEE JAMES 1:2, PSALM 103:2-5

DAMAGED GOODS

(DEVOTIONAL PAGE 169)

DATE:_____

Hi God –

So often the enemy tries to whisper defeat into my ear because he knows Your plans for me. He knows the only way that he wins is if he can talk me into quitting based on my past instead of pushing on because of my future.

I'm not going to live my entire life in the rearview mirror! I'm going to look FORWARD! That's why the windshield is so big and the rearview mirror is so small. I'm supposed to spend time looking at the future You have planned for me, not the past that I've already lived.

I'm not who I once was. I'm not my PAST. I am who You created me to be. When You came into my life, the old me was gone and the new me has emerged, because of You!

THERE ARE SOME THINGS IN MY PAST THAT I WILL NOT LET THE ENEMY HOLD AGAINST ME ANYMORE:

1. _____

2. _____

3. _____

I'm not going to look at myself, but to Jesus, whom You sent to redeem me, restore me, love me and save me. I might not be who I want to be, but I'm sure NOT the person I used to be. I'm not finished yet!

I have victory in You. I have an amazing future in You. My past is OVER and my future's so bright, not because of me, but because of You! Not because of what I've done, but because of Your grace!

WHAT KIND OF FUTURE COULD YOU HAVE PLANNED FOR ME THAT IS SO BRIGHT I'D HAVE TO WEAR SHADES?

1. _____

2. _____

3. _____

You have a hope and future planned for me that are bigger and better than I can dream. You truly did create me on purpose to accomplish things on the earth that are bigger than I can conceive right now.

I WANT TO DREAM WITH YOU ABOUT...

_____

_____

My Prayer Thoughts

_____

_____

_____

_____

_____

_____

_____

_____

_____

_____

_____

_____

_____

_____

For additional study, see Jeremiah 29:1, 2 Corinthians 5:17

• • ● ● ● • •

OBSTACLES OR OPPORTUNITIES

(DEVOTIONAL PAGE 173)

DATE:_____

Hi God –

I see obstacles. You see OPPORTUNITY for good, for me, and for glory for You.

I haven't seen with Your eyes, but I'm going to try. I won't look at what seems obvious as a problem and an obstacle, but I'll put my eyes and my faith on You. Not faith in the problem, but faith in the God that can solve every problem and make it an opportunity Who is beyond my imagination.

THESE THINGS LOOK LIKE PROBLEMS NOW, BUT YOU'RE TURNING THEM INTO OPPORTUNITIES:

1. _____

2. _____

3. _____

4. _____

5. _____

You say You will supply every need I have. Either You will or You won't. You promised that You will. Either I believe it...or I don't. I'm a BELIEVER!

Either it means "as long as everything is perfect, no one moves or takes anything away from me" OR it means "regardless of whatever happens, You're still God and You can have Your way no matter what!"

I BELIEVE THAT YOU WILL SUPPLY THESE NEEDS:

1. _____

2. _____

3. _____

4. _____

5. _____

WHILE I'M GETTING YOUR VISION FOR MY LIFE...

_____

_____

_____

My Prayer Thoughts

FOR ADDITIONAL STUDY, SEE ROMANS 8:28, 2 CORINTHIANS 2:14

SHAME ON WHO?

(DEVOTIONAL PAGE 177)

DATE:_____

Hi God –

The past is a place of reference, not a place of residency. It serves as a great reminder of Your grace and reminds me why I love you SO much. I remember what my life was like without You, and I don't want to go back. Look how far You've brought me!

You have taken my sins and thrown them as far as the east is from the west. You've FORGOTTEN the sins I have confessed to You. Now I'm free to run the race You intended for me. I will not be held down by my past mistakes.

I'M SO GRATEFUL FOR YOUR UNDESERVED, UNMERITED GRACE IN THESE AREAS:

1. _____

2. _____

3. _____

4. _____

5. _____

Everything that has happened to me in life so far has prepared me for this moment! I am ready to step into all that You have for me! Your future for me brings me hope! It's beyond my wildest expectations, and I'm following You!

SHAME OVER MY PAST MISTAKES ALMOST KEPT ME FROM EXPERIENCING THESE WONDERFUL THINGS:

1. _____

2. _____

3. _____

4. _____

5. _____

I'M EXCITED FOR MY FUTURE. I'D LIKE TO TELL YOU...

_____

_____

_____

My Prayer Thoughts

_____

_____

_____

_____

_____

_____

_____

_____

_____

_____

_____

_____

_____

_____

FOR ADDITIONAL STUDY, SEE ISAIAH 61:7, PSALM 103:12

I CAN'T PLEASE EVERYONE, BUT I CAN PLEASE YOU

(DEVOTIONAL PAGE 181)

DATE:_____

Hi God –

My reward is smaller when I go with the "people pleaser" approach. I may get a nod of approval from the boss, a friend, or even a stranger who I feel I have to impress, but that doesn't even compare to when YOU are happy with me. Pleasing people doesn't fulfill my purpose. That's why it never makes me feel satisfied.

HERE ARE SOME PEOPLE WHO I KNOW I'VE BEEN TRYING TO PLEASE:

1. _____

2. _____

3. _____

4. _____

5. _____

I can't control how people feel about me. When I run after the fleeting and fickle approval of others, I'm just chasing shadows. My only concern should be pleasing You!

When I please You, You tell me, "Well done!" You SMILE in my direction and I'm filled with purpose. You take me from where I am and give me the opportunity to do more!

I LOOK FORWARD TO PLEASING YOU MORE BY:

1. _____

2. _____

3. _____

4. _____

5. _____

THANK YOU, LORD, FOR CHANGING MY OUTLOOK. I'M ENTHUSIASTIC ABOUT...

_____

_____

_____

My Prayer Thoughts

_____

_____

_____

_____

_____

_____

_____

_____

_____

_____

_____

_____

_____

For additional study, see John 12:43, Matthew 25:21

DIVINE PROTECTION

(DEVOTIONAL PAGE 185)

DATE:_____

Hi God –

I'm so thankful for Your promise of protection! No matter how unexpected the storm, riot, diagnosis, hate, craziness, or terrorism might be... I know that I DON'T have to be afraid!

LATELY, THESE EVENTS HAVE BEEN MAKING ME FEEL NERVOUS:

1. _____

2. _____

3. _____

4. _____

5. _____

You can hide me, even out in the open, because I'm hidden in You. Trouble may happen all around me, but no problem, terrorism, evil, plague, or danger can come near me. NO WAY! Not in Jesus' name!

I can relax knowing that when I listen and follow where You guide me, I am SAFE! I have security and protection even money can't buy! What can man do to me with GOD as my defense? You have me covered!

I DECLARE THE BLOOD OF JESUS, THE HAND OF THE LORD AND THE PROTECTION OF THE ANGELS OVER:

1. _____

2. _____

3. _____

4. _____

5. _____

WITH YOU COVERING ME, I FEEL SAFE TALKING ABOUT...

_____

_____

_____

My Prayer Thoughts

_____

_____

_____

_____

_____

_____

_____

_____

_____

_____

_____

_____

_____

_____

_____

_____

_____

_____

_____

_____

_____

_____

_____

_____

_____

_____

_____

_____

For additional study, see Psalms 32:7, 91:2

REST, NOT STRESS

(DEVOTIONAL PAGE 189)

DATE:_____

Hi God –

You want me to come to You to release my cares and REST in You. If I believe in Your power, You promise that You'll be with me. Since You don't ever sleep, there's no sense in both of us being up. I trust that You're big enough to handle any situation that might come up. I will rest.

I'll stop overestimating my power to think of a solution or fix the problem. When I do that, I'm underestimating You. No matter what it looks like to me in the moment, You're already at work bringing all things together for my good.

HERE ARE A FEW THINGS THAT I'VE TRIED (AND FAILED) TO HANDLE ON MY OWN:

1. _____

2. _____

3. _____

4. _____

5. _____

You're the God of heaven and Earth, the Almighty God, my Healer, my Provider, my Peace, my Redeemer, my Savior and my Creator. You're the Alpha and Omega. You see the end from the beginning. You know how this all turns out.

Even though I can't see what's coming, You're already around the curve in the road, just waiting for me. You've gone before me into my future. You've set up provision, strength, wisdom, a way of escape and a way of blessing in that place that You know I'm coming to.

SINCE I KNOW THAT YOU'RE ALREADY IN MY FUTURE, I TRUST YOU WITH:

1. _____

2. _____

3. _____

IF I GIVE YOU WHAT I'VE BEEN WORRYING ABOUT, IT WILL ALLOW ME TO...

_____

_____

My Prayer Thoughts

_____

_____

_____

_____

_____

_____

_____

_____

_____

_____

_____

_____

_____

For additional study, see Psalm 127:2, Proverbs 3:24

STRONG IN YOU

(DEVOTIONAL PAGE 193)

DATE:_____

Hi God –

My strength isn't revealed in what I can do. My strength comes from overcoming the things that I thought I couldn't do but CAN with You! Your power lives on the inside of me. With You, I can do ALL things!

YOU'VE HELPED ME DO MANY THINGS IN THE PAST THAT I KNOW I DIDN'T DO IN MY OWN STRENGTH. YOU WERE WITH ME WHEN I:

1. _____

2. _____

3. _____

4. _____

5. _____

When the enemy looks at me, he sees that I have the strength of the angel armies behind me. I will never face a problem alone. Your angels surround me and hold me up so I won't even dash my foot against a stone!

I'm not of this world. I'm a CITIZEN of Your kingdom. You're on the inside of me, and nothing in this world is bigger than You! You do things through me that I could never do on my own. With You, NOTHING is impossible!

WITH YOU ON MY SIDE, I WILL CALL THESE IMPOSSIBLE THINGS POSSIBLE:

1. _____

2. _____

3. _____

4. _____

5. _____

HELP ME BE A POSSIBILITY THINKER. STRETCH ME. I'M EXCITED TO DREAM ABOUT...

_____

_____

My Prayer Thoughts

_____

_____

_____

_____

_____

_____

_____

_____

_____

_____

_____

_____

_____

_____

FOR ADDITIONAL STUDY, SEE PSALM 34:7, HEBREWS 13:5

CONTAGIOUS THANKFULNESS

(DEVOTIONAL PAGE 197)

DATE:_____

Hi God –

I always knew that the flu was contagious but I never considered the fact that being CRABBY is an attitude virus that can be more miserable than the flu. When I let my thoughts run crazy, it's no wonder I start to gripe! Complaining doesn't compel You it REPELS You! How in the world are You going to act on my behalf if I'm spraying "God-repellent" everywhere with my mouth?

I ADMIT THAT I'VE BEEN COMPLAINING ABOUT:

1. _____

2. _____

3. _____

4. _____

5. _____

I know the enemy tries to DISTRACT me with every little piece of junk. He tries to keep me from giving You praise. He knows that when I praise You, when I bother to take the time to be thankful, it pleases You.

When I thank You, it shows my trust in You. It calms my soul because I realize I'm not alone. It takes my focus off of my challenges and turns it to the GOOD You've done for me. I will not take You for granted because my thankful thoughts determine my mood.

MY THOUGHTS DETERMINE MY ATTITUDE, AND MY ATTITUDE DETERMINES MY ALTITUDE. I WILL THINK ABOUT THE TIME YOU:

1. _____

2. _____

3. _____

4. _____

5. _____

I HAVE SO MUCH TO BE THANKFUL FOR. I WON'T OVERLOOK IT ANYMORE. GOD, THANK YOU FOR...

_____

_____

My Prayer Thoughts

_____

_____

_____

_____

_____

_____

_____

_____

_____

_____

_____

_____

_____

_____

_____

_____

_____

_____

_____

_____

_____

_____

_____

_____

_____

_____

_____

For additional study, see Hebrews 12:28, 13:15

IN THE FIGHT

(DEVOTIONAL PAGE 201)

DATE:_____

Hi God –

When I think about all the hits I've taken on the chin, I always picture myself standing there alone. The truth of the matter is, You were always right there WITH me. I have to tag You in. I have to give You a shot at the fight. You're a gentlemen who will not step in unless You're asked.

Your Word says to "fight the good fight of faith." But I don't have to fight alone. I believe that You CAN and You WILL finish the fight for me. That You'll sustain me to the end. It's not just me in the ring; it's You and me. You're there to fight the battle, but the victory is mine!

HERE ARE A FEW PROBLEMS THAT I'VE BEEN FIGHTING WITH:

1. _____

2. _____

3. _____

4. _____

5. _____

I know I'm not enough on my own. But I'm NOT alone. I don't have to be afraid anymore. You're with me. You comfort me. You restore me. You empower me. You lift me up! You charge me up!

You increase my strength, multiply my confidence, and make power and might ABOUND in anyone who has their hope in You...and that's me!

I CAN SEE THESE VICTORIES ON THE HORIZON:

1. _____

2. _____

3. _____

4. _____

5. _____

I'M READY TO TALK, TO DREAM, TO HEAR
FROM YOU ABOUT...

_____

_____

My Prayer Thoughts

FOR ADDITIONAL STUDY, SEE PSALMS 23:4, 28:7

TAKE TODAY BACK

(DEVOTIONAL PAGE 205)

DATE:_____

Hi God –

The enemy didn't make today. You did! THIS is the day the LORD has made. You made THIS particular day for ME. You didn't make this day to defeat me. You made this day as an opportunity for me to lean into You, to trust You and to follow You.

The Bible gives me a COMMAND about what to do today. I WILL rejoice and be GLAD in today. I will not be defeated by what I see with my natural eyes.

BLESS THE LORD, OH MY SOUL, AND ALL THAT IS WITHIN ME. BLESS HIS HOLY NAME. SOUL...WE HAVE SOME WORK TO DO, SO LET'S GET TO IT! LORD, I WILL BLESS YOU BY:

1. _____

2. _____

3. _____

4. _____

5. _____

Lord, You command me in this because You know I need to reign in my emotions. I will get out of fear in my natural mind and get into faith. Faith pleases You. And when You're happy with me, when I'm obedient and follow You, You'll take me to a good place!

THESE ARE GOOD PLACES THAT I IMAGINE YOU'RE TAKING ME:

1. _____

2. _____

3. _____

4. _____

5. _____

THANK YOU FOR ALWAYS LISTENING TO ME. I WANT TO TELL YOU...

_____

_____

My Prayer Thoughts

_____

_____

_____

_____

_____

_____

_____

_____

_____

_____

_____

_____

_____

FOR ADDITIONAL STUDY, SEE PSALM 103:1-2, MARK 11:22

I'M IN TROUBLE

(DEVOTIONAL PAGE 209)

DATE:_____

Hi God –

In Psalms, it says that the poor man cried out and You heard him and SAVED him from all of his troubles. I have trouble too. I was just thinking, *Poor little me.*

Your Word says that You are not partial to people. What You do for one person. You'll do for me! You saved the poor man, and I believe You will save me, too!

You promise that if I seek You, You will answer me and deliver me from all my fears. Here I am, God! I'm SEEKING You, I'm believing in You, I'm trusting You, I'm listening for You, and I'm obedient to anything that You would have me do.

LORD, HELP ME! HERE'S WHERE I'M IN TROUBLE:

1. _____

2. _____

3. _____

4. _____

5. _____

You're not a God that is moved by need. You're moved by FAITH. When I cry out, You hear me!

I cry out in FAITH: faith in You and Your everlasting kindness and faith in Your unfathomable grace. Grace—it's undeserved, unwarranted FAVOR! It's something I can't earn and I'll never deserve. It's just a FREE gift from You. You give the best gifts!

I WILL MAKE SOME FAITH STATEMENTS, RIGHT NOW. BY FAITH I BELIEVE...

1. _____

2. _____

3. _____

THANK YOU FOR ALWAYS LISTENING TO ME. I WANT TO TELL YOU...

_____

_____

_____

My Prayer Thoughts

_____

_____

_____

_____

_____

_____

_____

_____

_____

_____

_____

_____

_____

_____

_____

_____

_____

_____

_____

_____

_____

_____

_____

_____

_____

_____

FOR ADDITIONAL STUDY, SEE PSALM 18:6, 1 CORINTHIANS 10:13

WHEN LIFE THROWS ME LEMONS

(DEVOTIONAL PAGE 213)

DATE:_____

Hi God —

Letting the situation determine what happens to me is NOT faith. It's the opposite of faith and will actually pull me into defeat. I can't allow things to stop me. Instead, I turn that into the very reason that I WON'T stop. What I see now is only temporary and subject to change. I'm putting in a change order!

IN JESUS' NAME, HERE ARE SOME AFFAIRS THAT I'M ORDERING TO CHANGE:

1. _____

2. _____

3. _____

4. _____

5. _____

Your Word says that with You, I will ALWAYS have victory. You are causing me to come out on top, no matter what the enemy throws at me. You've empowered me to be the head and not the tail, and to be above and not beneath.

The Word says, "The battle is the Lord's and the victory is MINE!" So I declare today a day of victory. Regardless of the circumstances I see with my natural eyes, I close my eyes and begin to see with my eyes of faith, my eyes of trust in God, and my eyes of victory! And by the way, devil, you can have your lemons back. I ordered espresso!

SOME SOUR MOMENTS THAT GOD IS TURNING INTO DELICIOUS ESPRESSO FOR ME:

1. _____

2. _____

3. _____

4. _____

MY TRUST IN YOU GROWS DAY BY DAY ABOUT...

_____

_____

My Prayer Thoughts

_____

_____

_____

_____

_____

_____

_____

_____

_____

_____

_____

_____

_____

For additional study, see Genesis 50:20, 2 Corinthians 4:8-9

I'M GETTING ANTSY

(DEVOTIONAL PAGE 217)

DATE:_____

Hi God –

I'm ready. I mean, I THINK I'm ready. What am I saying? Just bless me already! I've got a whole list of things I need for You to do:

MY GOD TO-DO LIST INCLUDES:

1. _____

2. _____

3. _____

4. _____

5. _____

I know I want it now. But just because victory isn't happening this very moment, that does NOT mean the win isn't coming!

You tell me to wait on You to move. I prefer to find the speed-pass fast-track lane. But that's not how You work. It isn't about me; it's about You. When I wait on You, the benefits are bizarre and beyond natural understanding or comprehension. They aren't achievable by me alone but do-able ALL DAY for You!

God, no matter how the world presses me or people make fun of me, I'm WAITING on You. You are good. You bring blessing. You renew my strength. You're a miracle-working God, the God of more-than-enough. I trust You. I believe in You! I will wait on You!

THE BENEFITS OF WAITING ON YOU ARE:

1. _____

2. _____

3. _____

4. _____

5. _____

WHILE I WAIT ON YOU, I'D LIKE TO SHARE...

_____

_____

_____

My Prayer Thoughts

_____

_____

_____

_____

_____

_____

_____

_____

_____

_____

_____

_____

_____

FOR ADDITIONAL STUDY, SEE PSALM 46:10, ISAIAH 30:18

I DON'T KNOW WHAT TO DO

(DEVOTIONAL PAGE 221)

DATE:_____

Hi God –

I feel like I'm in a FOG! I can't see which way to go and the sun is setting on my opportunity. Just because twilight comes and things start to get dark, it doesn't mean I have to stay in the dark. I will know what to do when the time comes. Darkness just gives me an opportunity to see the power of Your light.

I'm not afraid, because I know what to do. I go to You in prayer. I ask You for wisdom. I ask You what to do and You gladly tell me. The Bible says You're always ready to give a bountiful supply of wisdom to ANYONE who asks. The Word says You give wisdom liberally. I receive Your gift of wisdom!

I NEED YOUR WISDOM TO KNOW WHAT I SHOULD DO ABOUT:

1. _____

2. _____

3. _____

4. _____

God, You're waiting for me to call on You. I've tied Your hands until I reach out. But now I loose Your mighty power. I call to You and You answer me. You show me great and mighty things that I do not know or understand.

You haven't even given me a dream that I can accomplish on my own. It takes faith to please You. I have to lean on, rely on, and confidently trust in You. I have to get to those places where I don't know what to do in my natural understanding so that I can go to You. That's when You are there for me.

HERE ARE WAYS THAT YOU SPEAK YOUR DIRECTION TO ME:

1. _____

2. _____

3. _____

I'M TRUSTING YOU, GOD. AND WHILE I'M OPENING MYSELF UP TO YOU...

_____

_____

_____

My Prayer Thoughts

_____

_____

_____

_____

_____

_____

_____

_____

_____

_____

_____

_____

_____

For additional study, see Job 29:3, Jeremiah 33:3

IN-CHRISTED

(DEVOTIONAL PAGE 225)

DATE:_____

Hi God –

Unlike me, You aren't interested in what I'm NOT: my weaknesses, my shortfalls, my failures or the things I get hung up on. You knew me before I was born. You know everything. You knew I would mess up and get things wrong, but You created me and love me anyway.

By being "in Christ," I get Your encouragement, inspiration, strength and wisdom. I get to be NEW. My past somehow doesn't even count. It doesn't register. All that matters is that I am in You, and because of that, everything has changed!

OUT OF CHRIST, THESE ARE THINGS I STRUGGLE WITH:

1. _____

2. _____

3. _____

4. _____

You aren't thrown off by my failures. You were with me when they happened. Not only am I in You, You are IN me. Nothing can separate me, untangle me, or pull me apart from You and Your love!

You're interested in who I am in You. You don't see me for who I am in my flesh. Now that I have made you my God and King, you see me in Christ.

When I connect to who I am in You, I connect to power, strength, grace, mercy, happiness, wholeness, meaning and purpose. When I step into who I am in Christ, my FAITH increases, my POWER increases, my WHOLE LIFE moves to another level!

IN CHRIST, I HAVE THE ABILITY TO:

1. _____

2. _____

3. _____

KNOWING THAT YOU SEE ME IN CHRIST AND HIS RIGHTEOUSNESS MAKES ME WANT TO THANK YOU FOR:

_____

_____

_____

My Prayer Thoughts

_____

_____

_____

_____

_____

_____

_____

_____

_____

_____

_____

_____

_____

_____

For additional study, see Romans 8:39, 1 John 4:4

• • ● ● ● • •

IN NEED OF WISDOM

(DEVOTIONAL PAGE 229)

DATE:_____

Hi God –

I feel like I should have the ANSWER to whatever comes my way. It doesn't matter if it's a curve ball out of nowhere. I still feel like I should be able to handle it. But sometimes I just don't know what to do.

I don't have to come up with the answers in my own mind or with my own education. I have the mind of Christ and the wisdom of God. And because of You, I can use knowledge correctly, because You give me Your spirit of wisdom and revelation.

You help me see things I've never seen before and in ways I haven't thought of previously. With You, I UNDERSTAND things at a deeper level. I have great ideas and keen insights like never before.

You show me things that I couldn't have otherwise known. You know ALL and share these things with me. When I seek You and listen to Your voice, You cause my words to overflow with wisdom.

YOU SHOW ME THINGS THAT I COULD NEVER THINK OF ON MY OWN:

1. _____

2. _____

3. _____

BECAUSE OF YOUR WISDOM FLOWING THROUGH ME, I CAN SAY OUT LOUD WITH CONFIDENCE:

1. I will make the right decision at the right time!

2. I will know which way to go, even if it isn't clear to anyone else!

3. I will say things beyond my own comprehension that will be a blessing to me and to others!

4. I will live longer. I will live satisfied and with honor!

5. Your wisdom in me will open doors, make way for opportunities, and take me places I could never have gone on my own.

WITH YOUR WISDOM AT MY ACCESS, I WANT TO ASK YOU ABOUT:

_____

_____

My Prayer Thoughts

_____

_____

_____

_____

_____

_____

_____

_____

_____

_____

_____

_____

_____

_____

FOR ADDITIONAL STUDY, SEE PROVERBS 2:6, 4:20

WILLING, NOT WORTHY

(DEVOTIONAL PAGE 233)

DATE:_____

Hi God –

I look around and see other people that seem SO MUCH more together than me.

You knew me before I was born. You KNEW how I would mess up before You even gave me breath. And still…You made me and gave me promises.

There were lots of "worthy" religious people in the Bible, but You chose the OUTCASTS. You chose Jacob, the trickster who stole his brother's birthright and lied to his own father to get it. You picked Moses, a stuttering murderer hiding on the backside of a desert. You called Saul, a mass murderer of Christians, to write two-thirds of the New Testament.

I FEEL LIKE I DON'T QUALIFY FOR YOUR HELP OR BLESSING BECAUSE:

1. _____

2. _____

3. _____

4. _____

I might not feel worthy enough to be used, chosen, called, healed or blessed, but I sure am WILLING! It's NOT my goodness that earns me any of these gifts. You bless me, heal me, help me, not because I'm good, but because You're good!

My willingness to be used by You will take me places my own worthiness never could! I won't wait to be perfect. I won't stall until I can try to put it all together. I won't delay because I think I'm deficient.

GOD, I'M WILLING TO:

1. _____

2. _____

3. _____

I'M WILLING TO TALK TO YOU ABOUT THINGS I'VE BEEN SHY ABOUT, LIKE...

_____

_____

_____

My Prayer Thoughts

_____

_____

_____

_____

_____

_____

_____

_____

_____

_____

_____

_____

_____

For additional study, see Romans 3:10, Ephesians 1:7

• • ● ● ● • •

WHEN GIANTS COME

(DEVOTIONAL PAGE 237)

DATE:_____

Hi God –

I see this GIGANTIC mountain! Sometimes I get distracted by the size of it. I have to change my focus and figure out how to keep from looking at the situation. I need to begin looking at the God who can build, move, destroy or make that same enormous mess beautiful!

I need to peel my eyes and ears away from the details: their words, the threats, the warnings, the news, social media, and the rest of the craziness. I have to focus on the Creator: my Savior, the Promise, my Redeemer, the One who has never left me and will never leave me. Father, help me remember that You are bigger than the problem.

HONESTLY, THESE THINGS I'VE BEEN LOOKING AT AND LISTENING TO HAVE ME RATTLED:

1. _____

2. _____

3. _____

4. _____

The mound of junk happening around me may have gotten my attention for a minute, but in comparison, Your power is LIMIT-LESS! There's no end to it. Either I believe that...or I don't. Is Your power limited? That's a yes or no question. If I take the time to remember what You've done, there can only be one answer.

You created the earth. You said, "Let there be light!" And light is still being created. The universe expands even though it's already 15.5 billion light years wide. When Your Word goes forth, it accomplishes that which You sent it to accomplish. It doesn't stop, no matter what it encounters. That is BIG!

I TAKE TIME TO REMEMBER THE THINGS THAT YOU'VE DONE FOR ME:

1. _____

2. _____

3. _____

WHILE I REMEMBER YOUR GOODNESS, I WANT TO TALK TO YOU ABOUT MY FUTURE...

_____

_____

My Prayer Thoughts

_____

_____

_____

_____

_____

_____

_____

_____

_____

_____

_____

_____

_____

_____

FOR ADDITIONAL STUDY, SEE HEBREWS 13:5, JOHN 10:29

NOT FINISHED YET

(DEVOTIONAL PAGE 241)

DATE:_____

Hi God –

I don't like to talk about it in public, but I have to admit that I'm a little ROUGH around the edges. I look around at other people and see how polished and together they look. I want to be like that.

IN THE CONFIDENCE OF MY JOURNAL, I CONFIDE IN YOU THAT I WANT TO IMPROVE:

1. _____

2. _____

3. _____

4. _____

5. _____

I have ideas about what I want to change about me. But You also have ideas about me.

You accept and love who I am. You see too much POTENTIAL in me to leave me here. You lead me into becoming a more loving, more compassionate, kinder, more peaceful and happier me. I can't do it alone. Self-help isn't enough or we all would've helped ourselves by now.

Jesus, not me, is the author and the finisher of my faith. You're the finisher because there is work in me that still needs to be done. God, if You can look at me as an unfinished work and say that I'm still good, I should be able to give myself a little GRACE. I just need to have patience with myself and allow You to keep working in me.

I'M A WORK IN PROGRESS, AND I'M OKAY WITH THAT. GOD, KEEP WORKING ON ME IN THESE AREAS:

1. _____

2. _____

3. _____

THANK YOU FOR ALWAYS BEING WILLING TO LOVE ME RIGHT WHERE I AM. WITH THAT BEING SAID:

_____

_____

_____

My Prayer Thoughts

_____

_____

_____

_____

_____

_____

_____

_____

_____

_____

_____

_____

FOR ADDITIONAL STUDY, SEE ISAIAH 64:8, HEBREWS 12:2